MANCHESTER TR

A Pictorial History of the Tramways of Manchester

by

TED GRAY

&

ARTHUR KIRBY

Memories

ISBN: 1 899181 06 7

Published by   MEMORIES T/A Castlefield Publications
    Dawson Street, Manchester M3 4JZ

Prepared by   Cliff Hayes, Northern Publishing Services,
    28 Bedford Road, Firswood
    Manchester M16 0JA
    Tel: 0161 862 9399

Written by   Ted Gray & Arthur Kirby
©   Ted Gray

Printed & *bound by*   MFP, Longford Trading Estate,
    Thomas Street, Stretford,
    Manchester, M32 0JT
    Tel: 0161 864 4540

FRONT COVER: A Manchester balcony tram on Wellington Road, Heaton Moor, c.1908.   *(Fac-Simile Series Commercial Postcard)*

BACK COVER: The Lord Mayor of Manchester driving preserved tram 765 on the opening of the Heaton Park Museum Tramway in 1979.   *(Photo: Ted Gray)*

THE AUTHORS

TED GRAY is a Founder Member of the Manchester Transport Museum Society, and currently Honorary Secretary. For ten years he was also Secretary of the Greater Manchester Transport Society, in the period which led to the foundation of the Museum of Transport in Cheetham Hill. His boyhood passion was the tramways of the Salford area, but interest spread to include transport history of the surrounding townships. Previous publications include *The Tramways Of Salford*, *Trafford Park Tramways*, *The Manchester Carriage & Tramways Company*, and two shipping books, *A 100 Years Of The Manchester Ship Canal* and *Manchester Liners*.

ARTHUR KIRBY has had a lifelong interest in Manchester tramways. He is the author of *Dan Boyle's Railway*, the story of the early years of the Manchester tramway system, 1901-06, Dan Boyle being the first Chairman of the Tramways Committee. Arthur has also written *Manchester's Little Tram*, an account of the single-deck trams on the 53 Circular Route, and *Middleton Tramways*, the history of the Middleton Electric Traction Company, 1902-1925. He is a long-standing member of the Manchester Transport Museum Society, which operates a working tramway in Heaton Park, using a preserved 1914 Manchester single-deck tramcar. Arthur was the co-ordinator and project leader of the volunteers who embarked upon the five-year preservation programme, which resulted in a derelict vehicle being rebuilt and restored to splendid operational condition.

The Manchester Transport Museum Society

is a registered charity which was founded in 1961 by the late Clifford Taylor and others. Its members are volunteers who, with the support of Manchester City Council, established a Museum and tramway in Heaton Park in 1979. The MTMS seeks to preserve any items relevant to Manchester's tramways, and consequently holds an extensive archive section as well as numerous small exhibits. Temporarily stored elsewhere is an open-top double-deck Manchester tramcar, number 173. Several large items await restoration, including an example of an Eades Patent Reversible Horse-Tram from the Manchester Carriage & Tramways Company. The museum tramway operates on Sundays and Bank Holidays from Easter to the end of September, using tramcars from Manchester, Blackpool and Hull.

For a more detailed history of the Manchester tramways, the following publications may be consulted :-

Dan Boyle's Railway	—	*A.K.Kirby* (MTMS 1974)
Manchester's Little Tram	—	*A.K.Kirby* (MTMS 1964, 1979, 1990)
Middleton Tramways	—	*A.K.Kirby* (MTMS 1976)
The Manchester Tramways	—	*I.A.Yearsley* (Transport Publishing Co. 1988)

INTRODUCTION

By an Act of 1875, the City of Manchester was empowered to construct tramway tracks along the main highways. The grooved, metal rails, sunk into the surface of the road, were designed to give passengers a smoother ride than was possible in horse-drawn omnibuses rattling over the cobbled streets. For the initial venture, Manchester joined forces with the County Borough of Salford, and the first line ran from Pendleton to Higher Broughton (Kersal Bar) by way of Manchester's Deansgate. Thus, both ends of the line were in Salford, with only the central section in Manchester. The Manchester length began at the city boundary at Albert Bridge (New Bailey Street) and led to Deansgate, thence outwards along Great Ducie Street, crossing the boundary once again at the Grove Inn on Bury New Road. In accordance with legislation in force at that time, the tracks had to be leased to private operators in return for an annual rent, usually fixed at 10% of the cost of construction.

John Greenwood of Pendleton had pioneered local horse-drawn omnibus services to Manchester's commercial centre in Market Street as early as 1824. His success had attracted competitors into the business, and by the 1850s services were offered along most of the main roads radiating from the city centre. In 1865 the various rivals merged their interests to form the Manchester Carriage Company. The Company then provided the public transport services throughout the Manchester area. In 1875, already having the necessary employees, stables, and workshops, and already operating the horse-bus services along the proposed tramway route, the Company was seen as the obvious lessee of the new tracks. However, disagreement arose between Manchester and the Company on the question of whether or not the Company should be obliged to rent *all* the tracks the Corporation saw fit to construct, for additional lines were planned once the first route was complete. The Company had no wish to pay rent for lines which were likely to prove unprofitable, and therefore preferred to tender for each route separately. The Corporation, on the other hand, wanted the Company to rent the whole system, or nothing at all.

In the event, the lease was awarded to Messrs. Busby and Turton, carriage proprietors from Liverpool and Leeds respectively, promoters of tramways in several British towns. They adopted the title '*Manchester & Salford Tramways*'. Services began on the first section of the line on 18th May 1877. The lessees had ordered 30 tramway carriages from the Starbuck Company of Birkenhead, but from the outset, by some secret arrangement, the Carriage Company provided the staff, horse-power, depots and stables. In the 1877-80 period, additional lines were added and subsequently the lease was transferred, the operator's title being changed to '*The Manchester Carriage & Tramways Company*'.

The original lease was for a period of 21 years, and thus due to expire towards the turn of the century. By that time the 1870 Tramways Act had been amended to allow local authorities to work their own tramways if they so wished. The Company, not knowing whether its lease would be renewed, made offers of improvements and carried out experiments with electric and steam traction, ready to modernise its undertaking if its future was assured. However, the decision was taken not to renew the lease. Instead, the Company's empire was broken up, with many local authorities in the Greater Manchester area choosing to own and operate their own tramway services, using electric traction taking current from an overhead wire.

Salford purchased outright sufficient of the Company's assets as were required to work the horse-tram services in the Borough during the period of conversion, but Manchester allowed the Company to continue to operate routes until each was ready for electric traction. The official opening of Manchester's first electric tramcar route, Albert Square to Cheetham Hill, was on 6th June 1901, with public services beginning on the following day. Thereafter, the number of electric tramway routes expanded, and the tramcar was in the ascendancy until threatened by the proliferation of motor bus services in the late-1920s. Tramway services declined as many were converted to motor bus operation in the 1930s, and the last Corporation tramcar ran in Manchester on the 10th January 1949.

In 1992 trams returned to Manchester via the first phase of the Metrolink system, which, though principally a railway service, has 1.73 kilometres of street-level track in the city centre, linking the former electric railway routes to Bury and Altrincham. There is also a 0.7 kilometre branch to Piccadilly *'Undercroft'* – i.e. under Piccadilly (formerly London Road) railway station. Further extensions are planned, and the city centre street section will remain common to all future routes.

ACKNOWLEDGEMENTS

For a pictorial history such as this, credit must be accorded to those photographers, known and unknown, who faithfully captured the local scene. Many of the illustrations are from the files of the former Manchester Corporation Transport Department (MCT), others are the work of early commercial postcard publishers. In the 1930s and '40s, a number of tramway enthusiasts set out to capture the declining years of tramway operation, and readily gave permission for their pictures to be reproduced. In many cases, their work is preserved today by bodies such as the Tramway Museum Society, the Greater Manchester Transport Society, and the Manchester Transport Museum Society (MTMS). Photographers to whom we are indebted include A.M.Gunn, and the late W.A.Camwell, W.Gratwicke, R.B.Parr, and G.N.Southerden. Illustrations are individually acknowledged where the photographer is known, and apologies are offered for any inadvertent omissions. For the MTMS, the work of the late Ray Dunning in seeking out and preserving items of Manchester's transport history is gratefully acknowledged. John Howarth of Eccles kindly assisted with the provision of a number of timetable advertisements from the 1930s. Details of the tramcar fleet have been extracted from data compiled by F.P.Groves, and printed in I.A.Yearsley's book listed below, a comprehensive volume which is acknowledged as the source of much general information.

By the 1890s the Manchester Carriage & Tramways Company operated over 500 horse-drawn tramcars on some 75 miles of track in and around the city. Most were of the Eades Patent Reversible type. Shorter and lighter than the original double-ended cars, the Eades cars were cheaper to build, required only one staircase, and needed fewer horses and less depot space. On reaching outer termini, a reversible car could swivel on its truck, obviating the need to unhitch the horses. In the city centre, routes were arranged to pass around terminal loops so that they did not need to swivel in the busy streets. The cars were built at the Company's Pendleton Works, where inventor John Eades was Manager. Most Eades cars could seat 41, 18 on longitudonal benches inside and 23 on top. In this example from the Openshaw route, a fare table hangs in the lower saloon window, listing the penny stages. Until 1888 the standard fare was three-pence, but thereafter short-distance fares were introduced. It also became cheaper to travel *'outside'* (i.e. on the open top) than inside. Tickets were not issued in Company days, nor were there any fixed stops for boarding or alighting, though it was not thought proper to halt a car on an incline where the horses might have difficulty in re-starting.

PHOTO: MCT

The 21-year leases of additional routes opened in the 1877-79 period were extended so that all expired on the 27th April 1901. By arrangement with the Carriage Company, the construction of the replacement track for the heavier electric cars, and the erection of overhead equipment, was able to commence before the expiry date. This example of an electric tramway junction is at Market Street/Cross Street. The rails are fixed on a bed of concrete, but the granite setts have yet to be replaced. A burden placed upon tramways by the 1870 Act was a requirement to pave and maintain the roadway between, and for 18 inches on either side of the rails. In 1870 it had been argued that the tram horses would wear out the stone setts, but, incredibly, this particular clause was never repealed, even though the electric tramcars made no use whatsoever of the road surface. Tramway operators were thus obliged to maintain considerable areas of the main streets for the benefit of others, including ultimately their motor-bus competitors.

In 1899 Manchester took delivery of six sample electric tramcars (five double-deck, one four-wheel single-deck) in order to assess their various merits before placing orders. One of the sample cars was constructed by John Eades at Pendleton. His son, also John, was appointed first Manager of the Manchester Corporation Car Works. It was considered that some 430 vehicles would be needed for delivery in the period 1901-03, the majority being of the four-wheel double-deck type. However, the total eventually included 100 double-deck and 25 single-deck bogie cars. Orders were split between the firms of G.F.Milnes and Brush. Car 331 is an example of the Milnes product. Fleet numbering began with car 101, the Eades sample car.

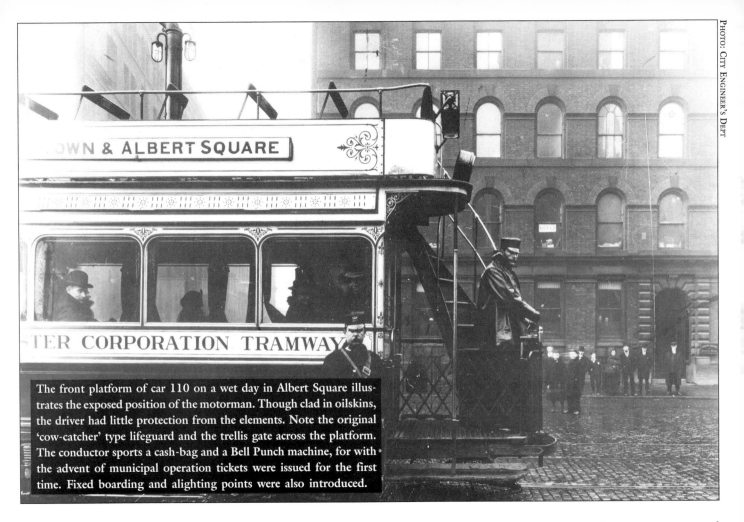

...OWN & ALBERT SQUARE

...TER CORPORATION TRAMWAY

The front platform of car 110 on a wet day in Albert Square illustrates the exposed position of the motorman. Though clad in oilskins, the driver had little protection from the elements. Note the original 'cow-catcher' type lifeguard and the trellis gate across the platform. The conductor sports a cash-bag and a Bell Punch machine, for with the advent of municipal operation tickets were issued for the first time. Fixed boarding and alighting points were also introduced.

◄ During the period of conversion from horse-drawn to electric operation it was possible to see both forms of traction side-by-side in the city centre. In this 1902 view of the Market Street/Cross Street junction a Cheetham Hill-bound electric tramcar approaches from Albert Square, whilst horse-trams for Old Trafford and Brooks' Bar move towards Piccadilly.

PHOTO: MRS. F. GREENWAY

► Deansgate in 1901-02 with car 298 ready to depart for the Grove Inn. Until June 1903, Salford cars were debarred from Deansgate because of a failure to agree inter-running arrangements. In retaliation, Manchester cars could run along Bury New Road only as far as the municipal boundary at the Grove Inn. To maintain services in the other direction, from Deansgate to the Salford boundary at Regent Bridge, Manchester purchased 11 redundant horse-trams and 132 horses, with temporary stabling and depot accommodation in Elm Street, off Water Street.

PHOTO: MCT

A notice from the 1904 timetable, in which the word *'buses'* refers to horse-drawn omnibuses.

MANCHESTER CORPORATION TRAMWAYS.

Chorlton-cum-Hardy.

BUSES run regularly between MOSS SIDE (Prince of Wales Hotel) and CHORLTON GREEN via Upper Chorlton Road.

Manchester's first depot for electric tramcars was at Queens Road, Cheetham Hill, designed to house 252 vehicles on 42 six-car tracks which fanned at right-angles from the approach line. Notices fixed to the pillars indicated storage tracks for particular routes. Nearest to the camera is the 'REPAIR BAY.' The first section of Hyde Road Depot and Works, needed to house and maintain the large number of cars already on order, was in use by December 1902, but the full complex was not completed until 1905. Additional tramcar depots were subsequently constructed at Princess Road (1909) and Birchfields Road (1928).

PHOTO: CITY ENGINEER'S DEPT

A few horse-drawn omnibuses were retained from the Carriage Company in order to provide services to Chorlton, Cheadle and Northenden, areas where it had not been thought worthwhile to construct tramways, or where construction was pending. These were housed at the Chorlton Road shed, as seen here. Three Crossley motor buses were acquired in 1906 to replace horse-buses, but after protests, the horse-drawn vehicles were re-instated and appear to have remained in use until 1915. One example was preserved, and is now on display in the Museum of Transport, Cheetham Hill.

▲ From their beginnings in 1901 Manchester's electric tramways expanded to reach Ashton, Denton, Middleton, Oldham, Sale, Stockport, Stretford, and Trafford Park. In 1905-06 over 133 million passengers were carried. With the extension to Altrincham in 1907, the system was substantially complete. Most main roads had a tramway. In the days before traffic congestion, tracks were constructed in the centre of the roadway, the overhead wires often being supported by ornate poles, as seen here in Cheetham Hill Village. As the number of vehicles competing for road space increased, the centre standards became a hazard and began to be removed about 1909 in favour of side poles mounted on the pavement.

◄ Piccadilly in 1904, then as now, had its tangle of overhead wires, a necessary proliferation at an important tramway junction. Milnes car 298, on the Conran Street route, sports a new roller blind destination indicator, which extended a car's availability for different routes, though the tram in front still retains the more restrictive four-sided rotating box device. The Milnes cars were easily identifiable by the cut-away dash near the brake staff. White tops were fitted to staff caps on May 1st each year.

As services increased, additional double-deck cars were ordered, and in 1903 the first 25 single-deck bogie cars were delivered, numbered 512-536. They were intended for routes having restricted clearances under low railway bridges. The opening of various sections of track linking Queens Road (Cheetham Hill Road) with Seymour Grove by way of Belle Vue and Brooks's Bar, evolved into the circuitous '53' route. This avoided the city centre, and was known as the *'circular route,'* but, in fact, it was considerably short of a full circle. The route used a portion of Wilmslow Road, where car 524 is seen passing double-deck car 206. The letter 'D' on car 206 was an early attempt to display route information, for service numbers were not introduced until 1914.

By 1906 the 'circular route' was so busy that 35 tramcars were needed for its operation, a total achieved only by temporarily removing upper-deck seats and fittings from 12 double-deck cars. Consequently, 20 more single-deck cars were purchased, numbered 649-668. Car 666 is seen in later years about to pass under the low bridge in Stanley Grove, Longsight, clearly demonstrating the reason why the route was unsuitable for double-deck cars.

PHOTO: CITY ENGINEER'S DEPT

MANCHESTER
CORPORATION TRAMWAYS.

CHEETHAM HILL

PARCELS
DEPARTMENT.

In 1905 the Tramways Department began a parcels service, guaranteeing a same-day delivery in the city provided the package was handed-in before 3.45 p.m. Items could be handed to the crew of any service car, who transferred them at one of several collection offices established around the town. Special parcels cars ran between these offices several times a day, and the final delivery was made by a boy with a handcart. There were seven cars with van-type bodies for the parcels department. Car 6 was photographed in 1906 by The Polygon, Bury Old Road, on a delivery run to the Cheetham Hill office.

◄ (FAR LEFT) The unpopularity of the open top-deck in wet weather led to consideration of the fitting of top-covers. The first experiments took place in 1904, the construction of the *'balloon'* roof being designed to fit on existing tramcars without the need for reconstruction of the bodywork. The top-cover fixed on car 589 was deemed to be the most suitable, and approval was given for similar roofs to be manu-factured in Hyde Road Works.

◄ (LEFT) The 'balloon' covers were fitted to 50 existing cars and to the 50 new bogie cars (599-648) being delivered in 1905-06 from the Brush Company. The platform design adopted for Manchester cars was such that it would have been difficult to extend the roof to shield the staircase, or the canopy to protect the driver, without major and expensive alterations. The 90-degree turn of the staircase and the exposed position of the controls may be noted in this view of car 636.

▶ (TOP RIGHT) The crew of 'balloon' car 578 pose proudly for the photographer at the Hightown terminus, ready to return on the cross-city route to Brooks's Bar via Junction, the latter being a spot in Hulme with a public house of that name. The third member of crew, the trolley boy, was a luxury seemingly indulged only by Manchester and Salford. Originally devised to combat unemployment amongst the young, the appointment proved to be a training-ground for future guards and drivers. Duties included the supervision of boarding and alighting passengers, bell signals, destination displays, and, of course, turning the trolley at termini.

▶ (BOTTOM RIGHT) The long route to Altrincham opened in 1907. 'Balloon' car 626 stands at the end of the line, trolley turned ready for its journey back to Manchester. Note the cast-iron horse-trough and the drinking fountain, once common sights at major junctions. The cab horse enjoys his fodder in a slack period.

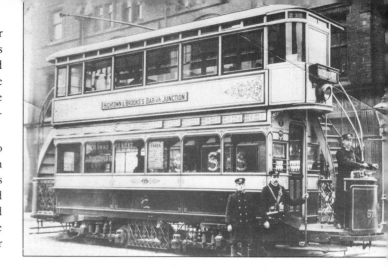

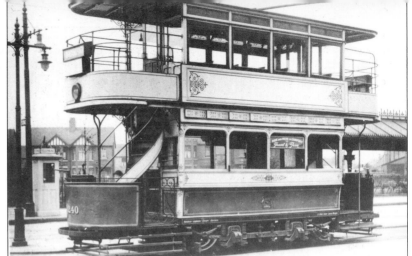

▲ After completing the 'balloon' top-covers for the bogie cars, attention turned to the question of similar treatment for the smaller cars. To give protection to those passengers who preferred to travel in the open air, a balcony-type cover was favoured. This time the conversion was much more thorough, involving the provision of longer platforms, new 180-degree staircases, and extended canopies, which latter alteration also increased the seating capacity. Some 95 four-wheel cars were so altered in the 1906-08 period, and orders were given for a similar design of top-cover for 25 bogie cars.

◀ In 1909 the Hyde Road Works commenced a three-year programme of building complete tramcar bodies, 11 four-wheelers (669-679) and 38 large bogie-cars (680-717). All were designed to have top-covers of the balcony type. With the introduction of route numbers in 1914, car 701 was the recipient of an experimental stencil-plate holder, adorned with wrought-iron surrounds. Evidently the circular design was not approved, possibly because it was more difficult to store and issue the plates, for it was discarded in favour of the rectangular pattern.

▶(RIGHT) Car 510, originally a Milnes open-top car of 1903, is shown as rebuilt with canopy top-cover and sporting the more usual type of service number, mounted immediately below the destination indicator. The provision of service numbers supplemented the route information carried on boards mounted on the top-deck sides.

▶(FAR RIGHT) Appointments to the traffic staff were exclusively male until well into the First World War, when so many men having joined the forces, conductresses were employed for the first time. The ladies were not universally welcomed - many thought they were taking the jobs of those who had enlisted, and demanded that they be dismissed as soon as the men returned from the war. A young 'clippie' poses with the motorman on car 731, a single-truck car new in 1913.

PHOTO: MCT

◀ One of the large bogie-cars, number 697, built at Hyde Road in 1911-12, mounted on Brush 22E trucks, and fitted with British Thomson-Houston electrical equipment, stands in Bowes Street at the side of Princess Road Depot. On cars built after mid-1913, the position of the headlamp was changed from the top-deck end to the middle of the platform dash-plate.

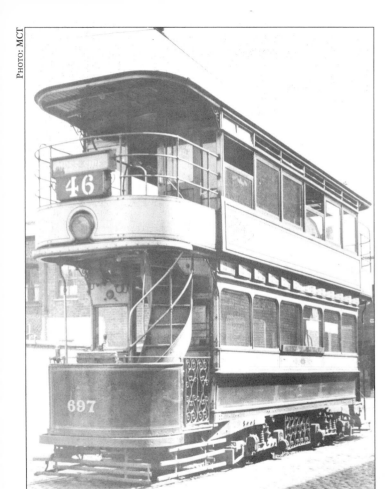

◀ In 1901-03 the earliest cars had been equipped with the 'cow-catcher' type wire mesh lifeguard, but these were replaced and all subsequent additions to the fleet were fitted with a locally-produced device. The Hudson & Bowring lifeguard consisted of a swinging gate which, when meeting an obstruction, cut off power and caused a tray to drop on to the track. Spaces between the side bogies were protected by wrought-iron 'dog gates.'

Manchester's first totally-enclosed tramcar was a 1919 rebuild of one of the 40 remaining open-top bogie-cars. The rebuild incorporated vestibules round both the platforms and top-deck-ends. After inspection, it was decided that all future new cars and all rebuilds would be to a similar pattern, giving a distinctive 'Manchester' style. More cars were converted to this design, one of the earliest in 1919-20 being number 198, seen here on the left in this view of Oxford Street in the 1920s.

PHOTO: NATIONAL RAILWAY MUSEUM

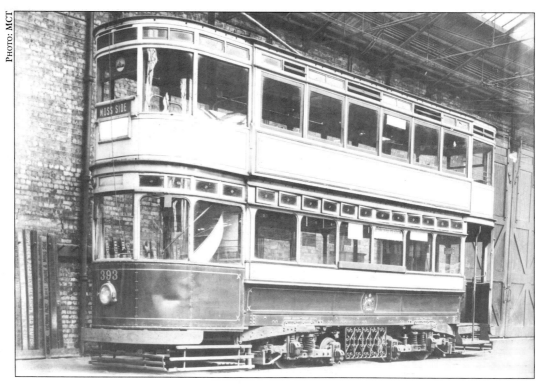

In the post-war years, more new bogie-cars were ordered from the English Electric Company. In addition, the Hyde Road Car Works continued to construct bodies. All were mounted on Brush 22E trucks. The fleet totalled over 800 vehicles by 1922. However, the earliest members of the fleet were by then over 20 years old, and some were in poor condition. The first replacement car, as distinct from a rebuild, was car 393, dating from March 1924. Similar in appearance to the new cars being turned out from the Hyde Road Works since 1920, the lower deck was new, but the top-deck was a flat-roof rebuild of the cover removed from the original single-truck car 393, but with an extra portion spliced-in to give additional length. More replacement cars of the same type followed in 1924-26. They were given the fleet numbers of withdrawn cars. Note (left) the route boards propped in racks against the wall.

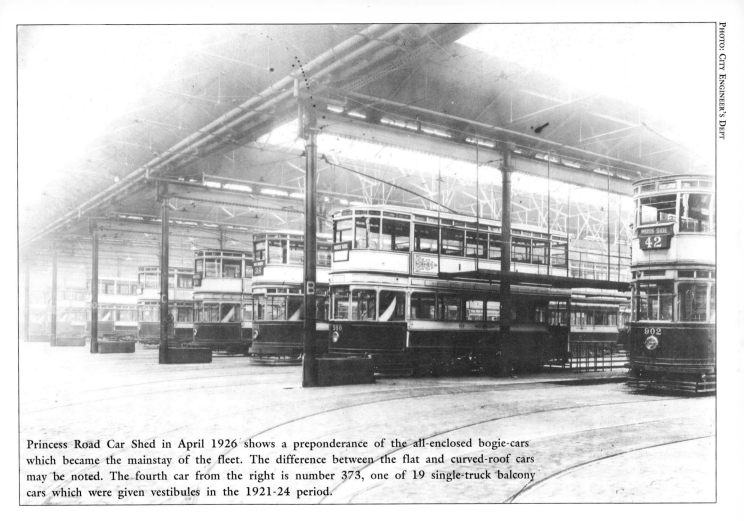

Photo: City Engineer's Dept

Princess Road Car Shed in April 1926 shows a preponderance of the all-enclosed bogie-cars which became the mainstay of the fleet. The difference between the flat and curved-roof cars may be noted. The fourth car from the right is number 373, one of 19 single-truck balcony cars which were given vestibules in the 1921-24 period.

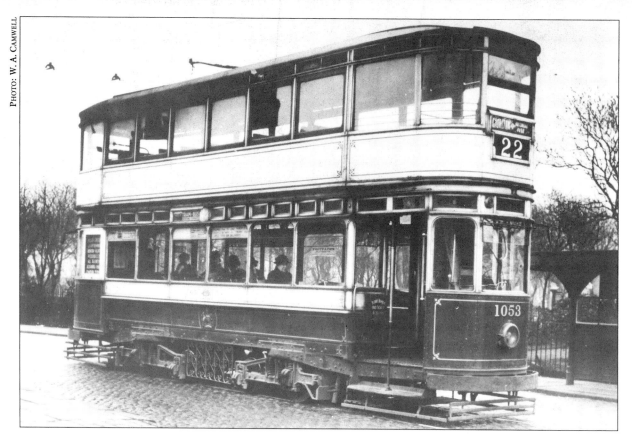

PHOTO: W. A. CAMWELL

The highest fleet number carried by a Manchester car was 1053, the last of a batch of 50 new vehicles delivered in 1927-28 from the English Electric Company. By that date, all the remaining open-top cars had been covered or withdrawn. There were still some 400 unvestibuled balcony and 'balloon' cars, but their combined total was now exceeded by the number of all-enclosed vehicles. Car 1053 is seen at Moston in 1937, ready to return on route 22 to Chorlton.

PHOTO: MCT

The last replacement cars constructed in the Hyde Road Works were fitted with wooden reversible transverse seats in the lower saloon, replacing the traditional longitudonal benches of earlier years. (INSET) Note the two-and-one arrangement, necessitating an off-set gangway, the ruby-coloured quarter lights, and the lamp-shades.

PHOTO: CITY ENGINEER'S DEPT

◄ PHOTO: MCT

▲ The Hyde Road Car Works continued to construct replacement cars throughout the 1920s. In this 1929 view along 'The Avenue,' the bodies of car 797 and others are stored on trestles at right-angles to those in the repair shop. To the left were the truck and machine shops, brass foundry, smithy and electrical department.

◄ The overhead travelling crane was able to lift and move complete tramcars. Car 806 is seen under lift.

PHOTO: A. WALSH

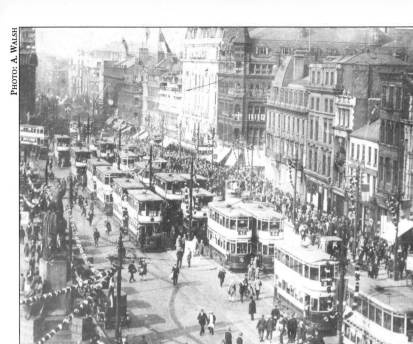

▲ As the number of motor vehicles grew, there was a proposal to relieve congestion by excluding tramcars from the city centre. The Tramways Committee understandably opposed such a suggestion. Piccadilly, decorated for the Civic Week celebrations in October 1926, gives some impression of the dramatic effect such a ban might have had. Amongst the Manchester cars are two Salford vehicles operating on the joint routes from Levenshulme to Kersal and Prestwich, the first of which had begun at the end of August 1926.

▼ In the suburbs, plans for rapid transit were realised to some extent by the provision of long stretches of reserved track on Princess Road (1925) and Kingsway (1926), single centre poles returning to fashion to hold up both wires. On the reserved tracks the tramcars were able to proceed speedily, unimpeded by other road traffic. Sadly, such provision was not possible in the crowded streets of central Manchester. In this mid-1930s view of Kingsway, the almost complete absence of motor vehicles makes the reserved track seem unnecessary for car 498 as it heads for East Didsbury.

SPECIAL CAR
20

266

◀R. Stuart Pilcher was appointed General Manager in 1929, becoming responsible for a fleet at maximum of 952 tramcars. The programme for 21 further replacement bogie-cars and 8 rebuilds was continued in 1929-30, the latest having the luxury of upholstered seats in the lower saloon. Pilcher, favouring the single-truck high-speed car, then switched to the construction of 38 four-wheel 'Pullman' cars in 1930-32. These replaced (and took the fleet numbers of) some withdrawn cars. Older cars, mainly of the balcony type, were being scrapped at this time, and most of the single-deck cars were withdrawn in 1930 on the conversion of the 53 route to bus operation. The new 'Pilcher' cars had a long wheelbase, with small wheels, high-speed motors, and a low-slung body. Having magnetic track brakes, the new cars were especially suitable for hilly routes. Car 266 was the first of the type to appear in service in May 1930.

Photo: G. N. Southerden

A number of the single-truck open-ended cars survived into the 1930s. In 1932 car 152 was captured working the shuttle service between Ashton and Denton. Note the unusual destination display. Evidently, DENTON did not appear on this particular roller blind, and the destination is shown on a printed card placed between the glass and the blind.

Photo: MCT

The parcels service continued, although in the 1930s the work was often carried out by motor van. Even so, firms wishing to have parcels collected continued to display a sign which read 'TRAM' long after tramcars had ceased to be used. In this picture at Chorlton, a parcel is being handed to the conductor of car 807 for transfer to the sorting office. Another useful public service performed by the tramcars was the late evening collection of mail via a letter box on the 'Post Car,' inward-bound on most routes at about 9.00 p.m. On reaching the city centre, the post-boxes were tranferred to the main Post Office.

The platform of car 872 shows a typical use of the under-stair resistance box – a convenient shelf on which to place the ticket box, and a useful spot to keep the brew can warm.

Well-used rails in the busy city centre were subject to greater wear than those in the outskirts, and consequently needed renewing more frequently. Before a major junction was relaid, it was the practice to set out the rails and points in the Bennett Street Permanent Way Yard, in order to check that everything would fit before digging up the street surface. This was the new November 1934 layout for St. Peter's Square.

▲ An oddity in the Manchester fleet was tram 436, converted in 1923 from its original open-top condition to a one-man-operated car, with front-exits located on the nearside (i.e. by the driver). It was used on the Stockport Road-Wilmslow Road shuttle service along Rusholme High Street.

◄The driver of car 891 stands on the fender as he fixes the trolley-rope in Piccadilly. There were various devices designed to prevent the trolley flying up in the case of a dewirement. One such was the 'trolley retriever,' a spring-loaded cylindrical drum on the end of the rope, which fitted into a socket on the dash-plate and kept the rope taut. Retrievers were tried in both Manchester and Salford, but fell into disuse. In the end, nothing was better than fastening the rope to some suitable platform stanchion or bar – the rope had to remain slack to allow for side-to-side swinging of the pole on curves.

The Piccadilly end of Market Street on a wet day in 1934 has a line of five all-enclosed cars waiting opposite Lewis's department store for the High Street junction traffic lights to change in their favour. Two horse-drawn carts are in evidence, but the number of private motor vehicles using city-centre streets is beginning to escalate.

PHOTO: MANCHESTER EVENING NEWS

A 1935 picture looks down on the junction of Market Street and Cross Street. Traffic moving into Corporation Street (left) appears to be at a standstill. Amongst the vehicles is one L.M.S.Railway house-removal container on a horse-drawn cart; a motor lorry carrying an alarming pile of sacks ; and a cart advertising *'Westmacott's Quinine Champagne.'* Would the latter two infringe today's safety and trade description regulations? Car 398 waits to advance to the Exchange terminus of route 19, the guard having already turned his indicator to 'HYDE' for the reverse journey. Behind it is a tramcar of Stockport Corporation on joint route 35.

◄A page from the 1936 timetable advertises the one-shilling 'Cheap Travel' Ticket, offering unlimited travel for a whole day. On jointly-operated routes, the ticket was valid only for the Manchester portion. By the mid-1930s more routes had been converted to motor bus operation, and the number of trams remaining totalled 755 in March 1936.

►A press photograph dated 20th April 1936 was taken to show freak darkness at mid-day. Car 113, followed by 832, moves along Cross Street with lights ablaze. Note the wooden indicator arm, hand-operated by the driver to warn of left turns, or the guard at the rear for right turns. These primitive trafficator signals were not fitted to all cars. The arms were not readily visible to traffic approaching alongside, and were easily broken. Most became disused.

Photo: Manchester Evening News

Tramway tracks in Manchester were usually double throughout. However, narrow streets in certain parts of Moss Side necessitated a single-track one-way system or, alternatively, single track with passing loops, as on Lloyd Street South.

▶ Joint workings brought Manchester trams into contact with those of other operators on several parts of the system. At Hyde Market Place Manchester car 424 working on route 19 waits with Stalybridge, Hyde, Mossley & Dukinfield "green linnet" car 63. The open-ended SHMD car is ready to return to Stockport (Edgeley). It has a fitting for a Manchester-style route number stencil, for until late-1935 SHMD cars shared in the operation of route 19.

PHOTO: W. GRATWICKE

PHOTO: G. N. SOUTHERDEN

◀ Other joint workings were to be seen on the two routes to Ashton-Under-Lyne. Pilcher car 274 leaves Ashton centre in 1932 on route 26 to Manchester (Stevenson Square via Ashton New Road and Droylsden), whilst Ashton car 12 arrives on a local service. The second Manchester-Ashton route (number 28) was to Piccadilly via Fairfield and Ashton Old Road. The Ashton blue contrasted with Manchester's red livery. In March 1938 trolley-buses took over operation of the Manchester-Ashton service, and Ashton's few remaining trams were scrapped.

PHOTO: A. M. GUNN

◄ Manchester Pilcher car 104 passes Oldham 125 on the hilly Waterhead section in August 1935.

PHOTO: W. A. CAMWELL

► Stockport's Mersey Square is the setting as Stockport 23 and Manchester 1035 wait to set off on their respective journeys. A large black letter 'H' painted on the dash of some Stockport cars indicated that they were low enough to pass under the bridges on the Hyde route. It was relatively unusual to see a service number displayed on a Stockport tram, but this one has the number 2 hanging in the top-deck end window. Stockport was the last town in the Greater Manchester area to abandon its trams. Some routes survived until August 1951.

◄ In 1925 the Middleton Electric Traction Company was taken over jointly by the Corporations of Manchester, Oldham and Rochdale, as a result of which Manchester acquired ten 1902 single-deck bogie cars, similar to the ones used on the 53 route. After some modification and reconditioning, six entered service as numbers 994-999 and one as 529, taking the fleet number of a withdrawn car. Three were scrapped. Car 529 survived the demise of the 53 route in 1930 to remain in use carrying bags of dried sand between depots until 1938. It is seen in Miller Street in 1937.

► A 1938 view of the three-track layout in Piccadilly, looking towards Market Street, includes a Stockport car and a new bus turning out of Portland Street. By this date, trolley-bus wires mingled with the tramway overhead, and the direction of travel on the centre track had been reversed to make it available for cars moving towards London Road. Note the clock on the facade of the Transport Offices at 55 Piccadilly.

▲ An unidentified Pilcher car braves the snow in Oldham on route 20 to Waterhead. Though the destination is obscured, someone has recently had a finger on the lamp, where 'OXO' stands out clearly!

◄ Pilcher car 266 threads through the Market Street shoppers as it turns into Cross Street about 1936. The destination is misleading. It is possible that the car was entering service on route 11A, Heaton Park to Alexandra Park via Albert Square. Car 253 behind displays a 37 black-on-white paper route number, a reverse of the usual stencil.

Photo: Daily Herald

In June 1938 problems of increasing congestion led to the introduction of a one-way traffic system between All Saints and the city centre. Inward-bound cars approached via Oxford Road, whilst outward cars left the city via Princess Street. The effect was to double the number of tramcars and halve the length of available track on these streets. In this rush-hour picture, the line of trams waiting to move along Oxford Road stretches back as far as All Saints, but the private cars are able to overtake easily by straddling the unused outward track. The one-way scheme resulted in disruption of the tramcar timetables, and further advanced the argument in favour of conversion to the more versatile motor bus. This was the last year in which the balcony cars appeared in service, and the General Manager proposed complete abandonment of the tramways within three years.

Tramcar drivers were not the only persons confused on the introduction of the new one-way scheme.
At All Saints, police officers were on duty to advise motorists. Three tramcars wait to move out
from Grosvenor Street.

PHOTO: D.ROURKE

PHOTO: MCT

▼ In the 1939-45 War ladies were employed once again out on the road as traffic staff. The majority were conductresses on buses, trolley-buses, and trams, but a few were trained as tram drivers.

▲ Tramcar withdrawals accelerated in the late 1930s as more routes were converted to motor bus operation. A June 1939 view at Chorlton terminus shows the rear of a newly-delivered Crossley 'Mancunian' bus. Trams 327 on route 23 (Chorlton-Hollinwood) and 1021 on the 37 (Southern Cemetery-Levenshulme) are working on two of the few remaining tram services. Route 23 was, in fact, converted in July of that year, but re-instated as a wartime measure in 1940.

By September 1939, only 450 trams remained, and had the abandonment programme continued, all would have gone within 18 months. Wartime shortages of fuel brought a temporary reprieve, however. Car 1018 outside Birchfields Road Depot displays the white fenders and headlamp mask required by the blackout regulations.

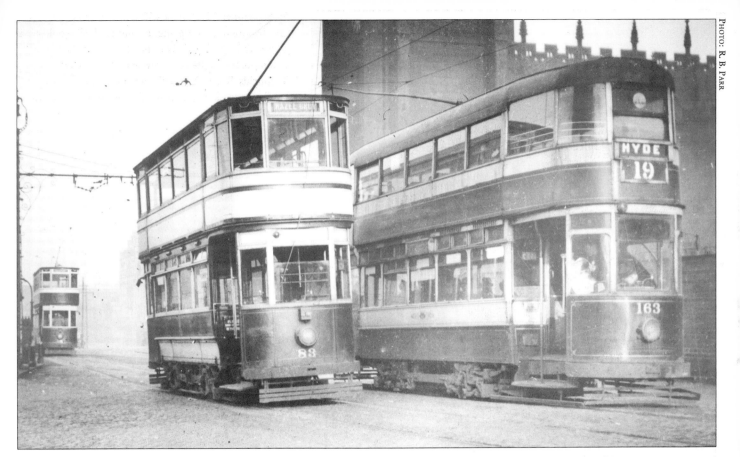

PHOTO: R. B. PARR

With the cessation of hostilities, and as soon as motor bus manufacturers could return to peacetime production, the tramway abandonment programme was resumed. Oldham's tramways closed completely in August 1946, after which Pilcher cars released from route 20 appeared mainly on route 19 to Hyde. In this December 1946 view car 163 shares the Exchange terminus with two Stockport cars.

45

▲ Manchester's last trams ran on the peak-hour Levenshulme service on the morning of 10th January 1949, after which there was a ceremonial procession from Piccadilly to Birchfields Road Depot. Employees gather round car 1007 in the depot. Through its windows can be seen the new Crossley buses which replaced the trams on the services to Levenshulme and Stockport.

▶ An ignominious end for Manchester trams. After the removal of any re-saleable material, withdrawn trams were scrapped in Hyde Road Yard. The exceptions were the 38 Pilcher cars, which were advertised for sale in 1946. All saw further service elsewhere, and all had left Manchester before the final days of tramway operation. Leeds bought 7, Sunderland 6, Edinburgh 11, and Aberdeen 14. The last two undertakings had previously been managed by R. Stuart Pilcher.

MANCHESTER CORPORATION TRAMWAYS: ROUTE DETAILS

Compiled by A. K. Kirby

Route numbers were not introduced until May 1914. However, for the purposes of this table, the earliest service along all or part of the route has been noted alongside the number eventually allocated. Numbers under 10 were not used ; numbers from 61 upwards were allocated to Salford, where they were not used until 1926. Many routes were subject to alteration from time to time, being lengthened, shortened, amended or absorbed as traffic required. Short-workings and variations were denoted by suffixes, 27H being the furthest letter reached in the alphabet. Dates of first and last **full day** of regular operation by tram are given. Several routes, or sections of them, continued to see part-day peak-period workings by tram after the date quoted. For example, workmen's services into Trafford Park continued until 24-8-1946, long after the regular tram service had ceased. Similarly, because of wartime conditions in the 1939-45 period, certain routes (for example, 13, 23, 38, 42F), or sections of them, were revived and returned to operation by tram.

ROUTE		FIRST DAY	LAST FULL DAY AND ROUTE
	Deansgate-Grove Inn (Bury New Road)	28-6-1901	30-4-1903	Grove Inn-Deansgate-Regent Bridge *(Incorporated in a Salford route)*
10	Hightown-Deansgate via Waterloo Road	30-9-1901	3-9-1938	Cheetham Hill Road-Chorlton
11	Cheetham Hill (Crescent Rd)-Albert Square	7-6-1901	4-7-1937	Heaton Park (Bury Old Road)-Alexandra Park
12	Hightown-Albert Square	7-6-1901	5-3-1939	Hightown-Greenheys
13	Hightown-Albert Square	7-6-1901	11-6-1939	Hightown-Chorlton
14	Singleton Rd-Albert Square via Cheetham Hill	18-5-1902	17-7-1926	Heaton Park-Albert Square
15	Heaton Park (Middleton Rd)-Albert Square	1-4-1904	18-11-1934	Greenheys-Middleton Road
16	Middleton-Middleton Junction via Oldham Rd	21-9-1903	31-3-1935	*(Merged with bus 54 to Stevenson Square)*
17	Blackley (Polefield Rd)-High Street	5-7-1901	12-11-1932	Rochdale-High Street *(joint)*
18	Blackley-High Street	5-7-1901	1-5-1934	Heywood-High Street
19	Denton-Piccadilly	1-6-1902	14-3-1948	Hyde (Broomstair Bridge)-Exchange Station
20	Waterhead-Piccadilly *(joint with Oldham)*	21-1-1907	3-8-1946	Waterhead-Piccadilly
21	Hollinwood-Piccadilly	1-4-1903	15-2-1931	Hollinwood-Stevenson Square
22	Piccadilly-Alexandra Park via City Rd	1-12-1902	27-3-1938	Moston Cemetery-Chorlton
23	Piccadilly-Alexandra Park	1-12-1902	1-7-1939	Hollinwood-Chorlton *(Reinstated 27.5.40-11.2.45)*

ROUTE		FIRST DAY	LAST FULL DAY AND ROUTE	
24	Kenyon Lane (Lightbowne Rd)-Oldham Road	7-3-1904	7-3-1937	Moston Cemetery-Stevenson Square
25	Bradford Road-Piccadilly	22-10-1903	26-10-1930	Hulme Hall Lane-Stevenson Square
26	Audenshaw (Snipe Inn)-Piccadilly	1-4-1903	30-7-1938	Audenshaw-Stevenson Square (as 26B)
27	Piccadilly-Old Trafford (near Seymour Grove)	9-3-1903	30-7-1938	Droylsden-Old Trafford
28	Audenshaw (Snipe Inn)-Piccadilly (George Street)	1-4-1903	1-3-1938	Ashton-Piccadilly
29	Stretford Road-All Saints	1-12-1902	17-2-1934	Trafford Park-Fairfield
30	Guide Bridge-Trafford Park	16-12-1908	4(?)-1-1936	Fairfield-Trafford Bridge
31	Fairfield Wells-Piccadilly	31-10-1904	19-3-1938	Fairfield-Chorlton
32	Clowes Street (Hyde Road)-Exchange Station	1-6-1902	17-2-1946	Reddish-Exchange Station, via Clowes Street
33	Denton-Haughton Green	7-10-1903		*(Absorbed into route 57 23-7-1923)*
33	Reddish-Swinton *(joint with Salford)*	19-9-1926	1-2-1948	Reddish (Bull's Head)-Victoria Street
34	Belle Vue-Exchange Station	1-6-1902		*(Absorbed into joint route 34 below)*
34	Belle Vue-Weaste *(joint with Salford)*	3-10-1926	24-7-1937	Belle Vue-Weaste *(joint)*
35	Piccadilly (George St)-Stockport (Heaton Lane)	1-6-1902	9-1-1949	Exchange Station-Hazel Grove
35B	Albert Square-Stockport (Mersey Square)	30-7-1922	15-2-1948	Albert Square-Stockport
36	Exchange Station-Heaton Chapel	2-8-1904		*(See joint route below)*
36	Levenshulme-Kersal *(joint with Salford)*	5-9-1926	1-6-1947	Albert Square-Southern Cemetery
37	Exchange Station-Levenshulme (Albert Road)	1-6-1902		*(Absorbed into joint route below)*
37	Levenshulme-Prestwich *(joint with Salford)*	29-8-1926	3-10-1948	St. Mary's Gate-Levenshulme
38	Longsight-Albert Square (via Plymouth Grove)	30-6-1902	3-9-1938	Albert Square-Chorlton
39	Stockport Road-Wilmslow Road	1-10-1906	14-5-1939	*(Un-numbered from 16-1-1933; see below)*
39	East Didsbury-Exchange Station (ex-37B)	16-1-1933	14-7-1946	East Didsbury-Exchange Station
40	Victoria Park-Hightown	19-4-1902	2-2-1947	East Didsbury-Albert Square
41	W.Didsbury-Royal Exchange (in via Albert Square)	1-12-1902	4-12-1938	West Didsbury-Royal Exchange
42	W.Didsbury-Royal Exchange (in via Piccadilly)	1-12-1902	12-2-1939	West Didsbury-Royal Exchange
43	Greenheys (Claremont Road)-Piccadilly	3-4-1905	7-11-1937	Greenheys (Wilbraham Road)-Piccadilly